CW00515845

BAD RECEPTION

A STAGE PLAY FOR TEENAGERS

PAUL VINCENT

Copyright, Paul Vincent 2006

Paul Vincent asserts the moral right to be identified
as the sole author of this work.

All rights reserved. No part of this publication may be
reproduced, stored in a retrieval system, or
transmitted, in any form or by any means, electronic,
mechanical, photocopying, storage or otherwise,
without the prior permission of the author.

British Library Cataloguing In Publication Data

A Record of this Publication is available
from the British Library

ISBN 1846850312
978-1-84685-031-8

Published January 2006 by
Exposure Publishing, an imprint of Diggory Press,
Three Rivers, Minions, Liskeard, Cornwall PL14 5LE
WWW.DIGGORYPRESS.COM

Note to Youth Theatres, Schools and Pupils. Although, broadly speaking, the author will be happy for this play to be performed without a licence or fee when it is being used purely for educational purposes, please email paul.humber@ntlworld.com in advance of the performance.

Notes:

In the original production 'Lucy' also played the parts of Wendy and Mr Mcfee.

A third actress played Miss Hitchins, Lavinia, Rick, the Driver, Mr Framlington, and the real Miss Collins.

If a male is added to the cast he would play Rick, the Driver and Mr Framlington.

If the cast is larger it makes it easier to cut some of the dialogue between Lucy and Kayleigh, which is often designed to give the third actor a chance to adjust or change costume.

ACT ONE

Lucy and Kayleigh go to a comprehensive school with a mixed catchment area. Lucy has an immaculate school uniform and Kayleigh does not.

There is a trestle table, a switchboard style phone and two chairs. A couple of parcels are on the floor near the edge of the stage. To this may be added further chairs elsewhere on the stage which are lit as further characters appear.

Kayleigh and Lucy appear from opposite sides of the stage. They are both on mobile phones and talk over each other at first.

Kayleigh: No. No lessons today. Yeah it's a doss. I have to do reception.

Lucy: Everyone has to take it in turns to do school reception?

Kayleigh: Oh what? I'm doing it with Princess Lucy.

Lucy: Oh gawd I'm doing it with Kayleigh Black.

Both wheel away.

Both: She's such a bitch!

They snap their phones shut and turn on their heels to face each other.

Both: (warm) Hi!

Lucy: So, which of us shall answer the phones, and which of us will take the messages to the classes?

Kayleigh: What?

Lucy: That's the system. Look they leave instructions. **(Picks up paper)** One of us works the switchboard and one of us walks around taking the messages and post and stuff.

Kayleigh: You don't need a system.

Lucy: (Pause) We'll share then. I'm Lucy.

Kayleigh: I know.

Lucy: We were in Miss McGill's in year 7? It was a few years ago.

Kayleigh: Yeah.

Phone rings, they both look at it. Lucy cracks first.

Lucy: St. Bloos. Lucy Houghton speaking, how may I help you? **(Listens)** So... so you want to speak with Miss Collins. The Headmistress? I'll put you through. **(Presses extension and puts the phone down)**

Kayleigh slumps back and plays with her phone. Lucy looks from the corner of her eye. She is keen to be liked. She reads the instruction list.

Lucy: **(Reading)** 'If you cannot read this please ask for a large print version at the school office.'

No reaction from Kayleigh. The main phone rings. Lucy sees that Kayleigh is not going to move and picks it up.

Lucy: St Bloos. Lucy Houghton speaking. **(Looks shocked)** Yes Miss Collins. No. **(Pause)** I didn't know that. I am truly sorry Miss Collins. Sorry. Bye. **(Puts phone down)**

Kayleigh is hiding a smirk and keeping her eyes on her phone.

Lucy: That was Miss Collins. Apparently we aren't supposed to put calls through to her this morning. She's in a meeting? We should put calls through to Mr MacFee, the deputy head? But not the Head.

No reply.

Lucy: She was all, **(Mimics Miss Collins)** 'Lucy Houghton, my instructions could not have been clearer:

Kayleigh: No no, it's more, **(Mimics Miss Collins)** My instructions could not have been clearer **(As Kayleigh)** Because she always sits as if she's trying to let one rip without anyone knowing. She's always raising one buttock off the chair and drawing her cheeks in with the strain. **(She demonstrates)**

Both (as Miss Collins): My instructions could not have been clearer.

Lucy: It doesn't say here that we shouldn't put calls through to her. Er... it says school uniforms should be worn. **(Cheering up, she eyes up Kayleigh's clothes)**

Kayleigh: Uniforms don't get much more worn than this. **(Pokes a finger through a hole in her blouse)**

Lucy: It says we should **(Reads)** 'answer the phone giving the full title of the college as St

Bloos Community College Regional Centre of Excellence.' Good grief. **(Shrugs. Eyes dart to Kayleigh)** You knew didn't you?

Kayleigh: Knew what?

Lucy: You knew we weren't allowed to put calls through to Miss Collins.

Kayleigh: (Mock innocent) I knew we were supposed to put calls through to Hairless Mac. Is that the same thing?

Lucy: Bitch.

Kayleigh clutches her heart as if someone has stabbed her. She has difficulty removing the knife.

Kayleigh: That hurt.

Lucy: Hairless Mac? Won't he be out on the sports field?

Kayleigh: He's got a hands free headset wotsit. For taking calls? They can't afford textbooks in this place but they can afford a state of the art phone system.

Phone rings. Kayleigh picks up the phone.

Kayleigh:(Lampoons Lucy's voice and body language) St Bloos, Elementary School for the intellectually challenged. Lucy Houghton speaking, am I connected to the person to whom I am speaking? **(Listens)** Yes. Lucy Houghton. L-U-C-Y H-O-U-G-H-T-O-N . **(Pause.)** Just putting you through. **(Clicks button)**

Lucy: (Appalled. Temporarily lost for words) Why are you doing this to me? We've been here two minutes and… . **(No reply)** You don't like me do you? You hardly know me. How can you know whether you like me or not? **(No reply)** Well I'm going to answer the phone from now on. **(Delves in bag. Brings out a text book and an A4 pad. She pretends to get on with work)** Who was that anyway?

Kayleigh: Miss Hitchins. The supply teacher? She wanted to talk to Hairless Mac. They're dating? Well they more or less live together.

Lucy: Miss Hitchins and Hairless Mac? Miss Hitchins? The one with the wonky eye and the piano teeth? They're dating?

Both: (Mimic Miss Hitchins: originally performed with a Bolton accent: her standard gestures to class are choreographed and performed in unison) 'My name is Miss Hitchins your supply teacher today, and I have certain expectations about how you should behave.'

Lucy: Hairless Mac though? Well I suppose he's got a certain something.

Kayleigh: Yeah, and it's contagious.

Lucy: How do you know all this?

Kayleigh: Me Mum does their cleaning.

Lucy: Your mum cleans up after Miss Hitchins and Hairless Mac ? Eugh. He's not exactly Love's Young Dream. I mean he taught my mum when *she* was here.... he's part of the furniture.

Kayleigh: Yeah, a stool. Shall we listen in to them? **(Picks up phone)**

Lucy dives over to put a finger on the switchboard.

Lucy: Nooo. **(Pause)** Can you really hear them?

Kayleigh: Yeah, you push that one then that one.

Kayleigh appears to be listening on the phone, but Lucy isn't sure and strains to hear. Kayleigh progressively pulls further away from Lucy.

Kayleigh: Boo!

The phone rings. It makes them both jump. Lucy keeps her finger in the button which Kayleigh then prises off.

Kayleigh: St Bloos Beauty School, centre of most excellent good looks: school principal Head Turner speaking.

Lavinia: (Lavinia is a charming menace: originally played like Prunella Scales in Fawlty Towers) Lavinia Sharp here, what is your name please?

Kayleigh slams the phone down. Lavinia looks puzzled and starts to redial.

Lucy: What was that?

Kayleigh: Lavinia Sharp. 'Pushy parent' She wants to get her daughter into this school because we get good results or something *stupid* like that. But the school's full in'it? Me mum says she's causing so much trouble, it's all the staff talk about.

Lucy: Yeah but why did you put the phone down?

Kayleigh: She'd report me to Miss Collins for larking about.

Phone rings. Lucy picks it up.

Lucy: St Bloos Community College, how may I help you?

Lavinia: Good morning again. My name is Lavinia Sharp. I was cut off before. I was in the middle of being connected with the Headmistress, Miss Collins.

Kayleigh cranes to listen as well. She pulls a look of disbelief.

Lucy: Right?

Lavinia: I demand to be connected to the Headmistress. I will not be messed about by a mischievous teenager whom it is entirely clear is abusing the trust of the school. I have connections at County Hall who would be most interested in my experience today.

Kayleigh: (Disbelieving) Yeah right.

Lavinia: I beg your pardon?

Lucy: (Solemn) Yes. Right. **(Pulls a face at the phone)** The trouble is I can't... **(Thinks)** Can I just put you on hold for the moment? **(To Kayleigh)** I think we've made her angry. Shall I put her through to Hairless Mac? It's what deputy heads are for.

Kayleigh: Yeah but she'll report me and... I'm... well I've got issues at the moment: I don't need no more trouble.

Lucy: Well you should have thought about that before monkeying about.

Kayleigh: (mimics Lucy) 'Muhnkeying abouht.' I know what we'll do. **(Grabs phone**

and mimics Lucy) Sorry to keep you, I think I have found a way to patch you through. **(Pause, then computer style silky voice)** Thank you for holding. Your call is important to us. All calls may be recorded for training porpoises. If you would like to speak to the school office...

Kayleigh passes the phone to Lucy who looks appalled. Kayleigh looks daggers at her.

Lucy: (Metallic voice) Press one now.

Kayleigh: If you would like to speak to the deputy head...

Lucy: (Metallic) press two now.

Kayleigh: If you would like to speak to the Head ...

Lucy: (Metallic) press three now.

Lavinia presses a button on her phone.
SFX Beep.

Kayleigh:(To Lucy) Shocker!

Lucy: What are you going to do now? Don't put her through! Miss Collins will kill us!

Kayleigh: I'll *pretend* to put her through.

Miss Collins (Kayleigh):   Sarah Collins speaking.

Lavinia: Good morning Miss Collins, it's Lavinia Sharp here, I wonder how we were progressing with the matter of admissions for my daughter Lucinda.

Miss Collins: I'm afraid there's been no progress at all.

Lavinia: It's just that I've been in touch with County Hall and raised with them certain discrepancies between the admissions policy as drawn up by your board of governors and the legal requirements as set out and formularized by the county education department. I have taken advice Miss Collins, and it now seems clear that I have room for certain legal action against your school... and you in particular.

Miss Collins: And good morning to you! And this legal action you are proposing. Am I to assume that it would, shall we say, disappear, if we were to admit your daughter to our school?

Lavinia: It may prove that upon further legal advice, my case may not be quite so much in the public interest as I thought. Anything is possible if you decide to *make* it possible, don't you find?

Miss Collins and Lavinia both make the same knowing simpering noise.

Miss Collins: I can't create spaces in my school that don't exist Mrs Sharp.

Lavinia: That may be so, but you have to

understand that I am only a humble parent concerned about getting the best for my child and as such I will be making your life a complete misery every hour of every day until you agree to take my daughter. **(Brightly)** Until later!

Kayleigh puts down the phone.

Kayleigh: Some people are just bullies.

Phone rings. Lucy fights Kayleigh for it. A teacher, Mr Framlington walks past with a pile of homework to mark. Lucy and Kayleigh both freeze.

Both: Morning Mr Framlington.

Mr Framlington: Morning girls.

They turn their heads in unison to watch him go. The fight resumes: Lucy then beats Kayleigh to use the phone.

Lucy: Saint Bloos Community College, how may I help you?

Rick: (Teenager, slouched cheek on palm, dead eyes, mouth half open, pencil hanging out of mouth) Yeah hello. It's Ricky Davis form 11.6, right? I'm on study leave right? Taking my GCSEs?

Lucy: Hi Ricky. **(To Kayleigh)** It's Right Ricky.

Kayleigh:(Shouts) Hi Right Ricky.

Rick: I was wondering right? I heard that when you're taking your GCSEs right? **(Pause)** If you get like a death in the family you get extra 5% on y'marks? I mean, is that right?

Lucy: You'll need more than 5% to take you from zero to even an E, Ricky.

Rick: Hey, I didn't deserve those zeroes for my coursework.

Lucy: I totally agree, but it's the lowest mark they could give you.

Rick: Yeah! Right! Well can you find out if that's right?

Lucy: Right. **(to Kayleigh)** He wants to know if he can get an extra 5% on his GCSE if he's had a death in the family. Who shall I put him through to?

Kayleigh: Who's died?

Lucy: **(To Rick)** Who's died?

Rick: Yeah well, right? I'd heard it's also true for like …pets?

Lucy: **(To Kayleigh)** It's a family pet.

Kayleigh:(Joking) 2% for a pet. **(Whim)** Depends on the size of the pet.

Lucy: What kind of pet?

Rick: Gerbil. But I'm very emotionally attached. Hang on, I'd like, get more points for a gerbil than, say, a goldfish, right?

Lucy: 1% for a rodent. Nothing for a fish.

Kayleigh: Tell him he has to send the dead animal in for certification.

Lucy: Yeah, right, Rick? You have to actually send in the dead gerbil.

Rick: Oh. Right. Like in a shoebox?

Lucy: Like in a shoebox Ricky. And before you take your last paper, not after. Otherwise how would they know when it died?

Rick: But my last paper's this afternoon! I'd better go.

Both put phone down

Lucy: Somewhere out there, in a dingy block

of flats where the stairwell smells of pee and leaking gas, an apprehensive gerbil solemnly awaits its fate... . Have those parcels been there all along?

Kayleigh: Yeah.

Lucy walks over to look.

Lucy: Looks like a delivery for Food Tech. Do you reckon we should take it down?

Kayleigh: Or we could eat it.

Lucy: (Holds the parcels) Tell me. Why *do* you resent me so much? I'm not posh or anything.

Kayleigh: What does your Dad do?

Lucy: He's just a lecturer. He teaches Classics at Queens College? We haven't got loads of money. I don't have a pony in a paddock. We don't have tiara wearing competitions every night in the lounge.

Kayleigh: Mmm. Tell me this. Do you have a cleaner?

Lucy: Look, we live in a part of town where the big school is exactly on the border on what you would call the posh bit and what I would call the council estate. We both get to go to the exactly same school. We both got exactly the same breaks. Get over it.

Kayleigh: Yeah, but you get to sit with the posh kids who are clever and I'm stuck in the bottom set with the chair swingers and window lickers.

Lucy: Kayleigh, we both started on day one in the same class.

Kayleigh: You're all la-di-da and no ass and you know it. You don't think you get any advantages but there always seems to be money for the school skiing trip, and when you do your coursework you've got broadband to nick stuff off the net, and then Daddy can whisk you off to Rome for your Classics, and can pay for extra tutors, and what am I doing in the meantime? I'm doing my paper round til eight and helping out cleaning at home because my mum hasn't got time because she's out... well, cleaning your house probably, so I don't get my coursework done.

Lucy: I'm not going to apologise for who I am. Anyway, I have got an ass, I mean arse; what's that about?

Kayleigh: There once was a girl with no ass.
She's a stuck up, posh, kind of lass.
I asked 'How dya crap?'
She gave me a slap,
And threw up two turds in a glass.

Lucy: You've been working on that since we've been sitting here?

Kayleigh: No *actually*.

Lucy: I'm taking these to food tech.

Exit Lucy. Kayleigh pulls a face. The phone rings. Kayleigh leaves it for a while then picks it up.

Kayleigh: St Bloos. Reception.

Wendy (Lucy): Hello, Wendy Houghton here. I wondered if I could have a quick word with the Head, Miss Collins? She asked me to ring her today?

Kayleigh: And to what is this appertaining to?

Wendy: It's a personal matter, about my daughter.

Kayleigh weighs this up.

Kayleigh: I'll just connect you. **(As Miss Collins)** Sarah Collins speaking!

Wendy: Hello Sarah, sorry to disturb you. Wendy Houghton here. Lucy's mother? You wanted me to keep you up to date with Lucy's problems?

Miss Collins: Lucy's problems? Abs-sol-lutely. So how are we getting on with Lucy's problems, exactly?

Wendy: Well you remember the matter we discussed last time?

Miss Collins: Refresh my mem-mory.

Wendy: What we were discussing yesterday?

Miss Collins: I get so many calls.

Wendy: Surely there can't be many people with that particular illness.

Miss Collins: No of course not. Let's start again. I am sorry Wendy I was being distracted by my secretary. Yes of course I remember yesterday. I do apologize, fire away.

Wendy: I've got the date for when treatment proper starts; which is this coming Monday and she'll be in hospital for three weeks, and even after that we have been warned that it is going to be a lengthy recuperation period, if she survives that is. But assuming the best scenario I am wondering if it would be possible for her to come in for half days and then possibly for her to have some work to do at home?

Miss Collins: I am sure we would be very happy to look into that. You will need to talk to her head of year though…

Lucy is walking back as herself.

Miss Collins: I'm terribly sorry, but I'm going to need to stop you there. Sorry. **(Looks puzzled at phone)** It went dead anyway.

Lucy: What was that?

Kayleigh: I was just getting myself in a bit too deep.

Lucy: You should stop doing that. Pretending to be the Head?

Kayleigh pulls a face.

Lucy: Who was it anyway?

Kayleigh: Who was that on the phone? Er... **(Looks at Lucy searchingly)**

The phone rings. Kayleigh puts both hands up. Lucy picks up the phone.

Lucy: Saint Bloos, Lucy Houghton speaking, how may I help you? **(Pause)** Kitchen's Direct? **(Pause)** Do we want you to quote us for a new fitted kitchen? You're kidding me? **(Pause)** Actually, the more you talk about it the more I think, yes, I would like a new fitted kitchen. That's something I would really like. **(Pause)** I tell you what though. I'm very busy right at this moment. So could you give me your home number and I'll ring you up this evening at your home? **(Pause)** Oh you don't give your home numbers out? That's because it's incredibly irritating being rung at home in your free time isn't it? Goodbye. **(Puts down phone)**

The phone rings again. Kayleigh picks it up.

Kayleigh: Saint Bloos.

Lavinia : Hello again. It's Lavinia Sharp. Can you put me through to the headmistress please?

Kayleigh: To what is this appertaining to?

Lavinia: The headmistress is expecting my call.

Kayleigh: (To herself) Now there's a fact. **(To Lavinia)** I'll just put you through. **(Pause. As Miss Collins)** Sarah Collins speaking.

Lavinia: Hello Miss Collins. It's Lavinia Sharp again. You knew you wouldn't be able to shake me off now didn't you? The avenue I am currently exploring is the exact distance to catchment area from my door to your school. I have discovered that a child admitted during this year lives in De Freville Avenue.

Miss Collins: So?

Lavinia: She lives at number 54.

Miss Collins: I cannot possibly comment on other pupil's situations.

Lavinia: Number 54. Have you ever visited De Freville Avenue Miss Collins?

Miss Collins: No I haven't.

Lavinia: Even though you live in the very next road?

Miss Collins: In that case yes.

Lavinia: If you were to visit that street, you would discover that in fact number 54 is not in the main part of the road at all, but in a cul de sac.

Miss Collins: Right?

Lavinia: I have visited the address in person and I can report that the property in question is a full ten metres further than number 14 where I live.

Miss Collins: What did you use a trundle wheel or something?

Lavinia: Never mind exactly how I…

Miss Collins: I bet you did. A trundle wheel! You walked up the path of someone else's house with a trundle wheel. Tell me Mrs Sharp, what is it exactly about our humble state school that makes you go to such extraordinary lengths to get your girl in?

Lavinia: Surely you know the strengths of your own school?

Miss Collins: Remind me. Is it the peeling pre-fab drama block with the leaky heater that is one spark away from blowing us to Hell? Is it the ice-cold swimming pool with the fungus on the wall that looks like a 3D map of Asia.

Lavinia: Buildings aren't everything Miss Collins.

Miss Collins: The alley where the smokers sit with the drug pushers from the nearest estate?

Lavinia: Miss Collins...

Miss Collins: The lesbian PE teacher who spends an uncomfortably long time with the girls in the showers? Or the teacher who leaves the answers to the SATs on the blackboard, but some of the kids are too damn stupid to even copy them down?

Lavinia: I'm sure this dates back to a previous era.

Miss Collins: Really? Then why am I sitting here with my pack of Seroxat and Whisky chaser, working out the number of days till I can ask the doctor for a repeat prescription without raising suspicion?

Lavinia: I can see I have called at a bad time. **(Ameliorative)** When would be a better time?

Miss Collins: There *are* no better times Mrs Sharp. This is my life.

They both put down phone.

Lucy: Oh you're good. You are good. How do you know all the stuff about the...

Kayleigh: My mum goes on about it all the time.

Lucy: Yeah, but you're good.

Kayleigh: Then that will be why I am being considered by RADA.

Lucy: Ah ha ha ha. The Royal Academy of Dramatic Arts?

Kayleigh: Yeah.

Lucy: RADA? Isn't that like a bit posh?

Kayleigh: (Posh) I can speak posh.

Lucy: Then why don't you?

Kayleigh: Have you even *seen* where I live?

Lucy: No, my mother and I drive through in our motorcade in the mornings with the car doors locked firmly from the inside and our noses held up so high we can't see a thing. Although I do notice the odd bump as we drive over the locals. So you're seriously going to change your accent if you go to RADA?

Kayleigh: (Cockney changes to posh during sentence) My accent'll change on the train down to London.

Lucy: But why RADA?

Kayleigh: Because you don't need A Levels and stuff. It's just auditions and nothing else.

The other places need A levels. RADA, you see, is like X Factor.

Lucy: Is that a fact? So it's either working in your uncle's chip shop or you're going to be a luvvie.   So you've gone for an audition at RADA already?

Kayleigh: Yeah.

Lucy: And?

Kayleigh: It went really well. They are going to call me if they want more auditions.

Lucy: Don't they say that, like, to everyone?

Kayleigh: No.   They don't.   But I've got a fallback. I'm also going in for X Factor.

Lucy: Okaaaaaay.

Kayleigh: They're doing a regional audition at Norwich? Next week.

Lucy: It's school next week. And anyway don't you have to be sixteen?

Kayleigh: I'll bunk off, just like I did for RADA. You coming next week? It's next week.

Lucy: Er. No. No I can't make it next week. Anyway, why would I want to go on X Factor?

Kayleigh: Everyone wants to go on X Factor. You alright?

Lucy: Yeah, why?

Kayleigh: You look a bit pale?

Lucy: I'm fine. Tell me. That limerick. There once was a girl with no ass. If you didn't make that up, then who did?

Kayleigh: It's just, you know, it's the rhyme everyone does about you.

Lucy: Everyone? Who's everyone?

Kayleigh: Everyone.

Lucy: But why? Why would everyone know who I am even.

Kayleigh: Everyone knows who you are.

Lucy: Why?

Kayleigh: Well there's your playing your violin thing in assembly and there's Miss Collins yawning on about your tennis every week.

Lucy: Cello.

Kayleigh: Whatever.

Lucy: So everyone talks about me and makes up rude stuff just cos I once played my cello in assembly.

Kayleigh: Yeah well you were just showing off.

Lucy: I'd just won a music competition. What

was I supposed to do, pretend I hadn't won? It's like that stupid thing at sports day where they give everyone the same ribbon for taking part. I mean, why race? We could all walk, cos there are no winners! We're all losers now.

Kayleigh: 'Oh look at me I can play the fiddle.'

Lucy: And if you go to RADA and you become a famous actress it's going to be 'Don't look at me, I'm not an actress?' What is your problem?

Kayleigh: My problem is you showing off. You happen to be good at something. Big deal! So you can play the fiddle, you can play tennis, it's not as though you're Serena Bloody Williams. You haven't the got the arse for a start.

Lucy: No. No. I don't *happen* to be good at something. I *happen* to work incredibly hard at music practice. Have you any idea how hard I have to practice? Hour after hour day after day? And for what? It's really only to please my parents.

The phone rings, Kayleigh picks up.

Kayleigh: St Bloos, Correctional Facility for the Community most excellent.

Miss Hitchins: Good morning, it's Miss Hitchins; can I speak to Mr MacFee?

Kayleigh: One moment.

Mr MacFee: (Lucy in the original production. Mr MacFee is an ageing sports teacher: ball under arm, and a football whistle stuck to his lower lip that moves up and down as he talks) Brian Macfee.

Miss Hitchins: Morning Brian; Rebecca. How long have we been dating?

Mr MacFee goes to talk but...

Miss Hitchins: I can tell you most precisely. It's been five years to the day.

Mr MacFee goes to talk but....

Miss Hitchins: I can tell that you've forgotten, 'cos there was no card or flowers. And I feel that this exemplifies a bigger trend these days.

Mr MacFee goes to talk but...

Miss Hitchins: For instance, I always treasure the yearly Teachers Conference; both Brighton and Skegness were most delightful in their way. So when you said on Tuesday that you'd not be going this year, I have to say that I have taken it most personally.

Mr Macfee goes to talk but...

Miss Hitchins: So Brian MacFee I'm telling you, there'll be no negotiation, I think that I will need to reconsider what we do.

Mr MacFee goes to talk but assumes he can't.

Miss Hitchins: Do you really have nothing to say Brian?

Mr MacFee: Yes. I do. I just want to say. I'm just waiting for a lad to take a penalty. I'm refereeing. Can you ring back later? Okay lads.

MacFee blows a whistle which deafens Miss Hitchins.

Kayleigh: How did you know about my uncle's chip shop?

Lucy: We do have friends in common.

Kayleigh: Yeah I often work for Uncle Rick, well he's not my real uncle; he has a chip shop in Croma? He says I can work there. Me mum says he's taken quite a shine to me and I should watch myself, but she doesn't know. It'd be nice to get out of this town. I mean, there's always something, you know?

Phone rings: Lucy picks up

Lavinia: It's Lavinia Sharp here. Could you put me through to the Head?

Lucy: Certainly. **(Hands phone over to Kayleigh and whispers)** Lavinia Sharp.

Miss Collins (Kayleigh) Miss Collins.

Lavinia: It's Lavinia again.

Lavinia and Miss Collins simper.

Lavinia: I've had a change of heart.

Miss Collins: Oh good.

Lavinia: I've decided I will take you to court after all.

Miss Collins: What?

Lavinia: I have been engaged in conversation with you many times over many months but today for the first time I have found your attitude most appalling. You were rude, unhelpful, unprofessional and…

Miss Collins: Then why do you go to such efforts to get your daughter in here?

Lavinia: What?

Kayleigh: (Panicking to Lucy) I've hacked her off so badly that she's going to take Miss Collins to court and then it will all come out that it wasn't Miss Collins on the phone and…

Lavinia: What did you just say to me?

Miss Collins: I want you to tell me exactly why you want your daughter to come here.

Lucy: Nooooo!

Miss Collins: If you can give me one good reason why this school is the best I will consider getting your daughter in.

Lavinia: Well there's the league tables.

Miss Collins: Fixed.

Lavinia: Fixed?

Miss Collins: We put all the brighter pupils in for general studies with two different exam boards to get an outrageously inflated points average. Never fails. Anything else?

Lavinia: There's your exemplary record on Special Needs.

Miss Collins: What, where we mark the worst idiots down as unable to write legibly and their answers are dictated to LSAs who then write down a creative interpretation of the answers they have heard. Bip-Burp.

Lavinia: Well, there's your glowing Ofsted report. I have it here in fact.

Miss Collins: I bet you have.

Lavinia:'A school that sets ground-breaking standards in how to get near perfect behaviour from even the most challenging pupils.'

Miss Collins: Ah yes, now we *are* proud of that one.   We have an arrangement with another school? In Ofsted week we send them our forty worst hooligans, in padded trucks obviously, and they send us their best pupils. We return the favour when it's their Ofsted. I'm amazed the inspectors haven't noticed the same bright kids popping up in every classroom in town straining their arms out of their sockets answering teachers' every question.

Lavinia: (Pause. Shocked. Quieter) Do you know who my husband is Miss Collins?

Miss Collins: No.

Lavinia: He is the Chief Inspector of Schools for the county.

Miss Collins: Is that a fact?

Lavinia: I think I've got some phone calls to make, don't you Miss Collins?

Lavinia puts phone down abruptly.

Lucy: Are you insane? You were already in trouble? You said you knew you'd made her angry. And then you just set about making it worse?

Kayleigh is stunned at her own behaviour, then gets despondent.

Kayleigh: Well I'm stuffed anyway really. I am on my umpteenth last chance at this place and...

Lucy: Yeah but you didn't have to get angry with her.

Kayleigh: Yes I did. Yes I did have to get angry with her. She's some horrible aggressive middle class bitch who, mark my words, will get her way and get her horrible little brat in here, and she has just cost me my place in this school. When my Dad came in here to try and sort out the Head do you know what they did?

Lucy shrugs

Kayleigh: They called the police! And yeah I'm sure they were right to call the police because my Dad's an idiot and he shouts a lot, but he's no worse than that woman, and they won't call the police because *that* woman is harassing Miss Collins, but she *is* harassing her; the only difference is she knows how to do it. **(Pause. Worried.)** It's not actually against the law what I did is it? It'll kill my mum if we have another court case.

Lucy: Illegal? Impersonating a headmistress? The last two occupants of the job did a worst impersonation than you, so I'd say no.

Kayleigh: Oh I've had it. A lifetime of working

in a chippy. How grim is that? Never getting the smell of fish out your hair not matter how you scrub.

Lucy: RADA might have you?

Kayleigh: Yeah right.

Lucy: X Factor?

Kayleigh: Do I look like Simon Cowell's type? Sharon only likes the boys. That just leaves me flirting with Louis Walsh. That's even grimmer than working in a chip shop in Croma.

A delivery Driver appears with a wrapped shoebox.

Driver: Sign for this?

Lucy reads the form she's signing then goes to sign, but Kayleigh has been looking at the box.

Kayleigh: Noooooooooooooooooooooo!

Kayleigh pushes Lucy away from the form and takes the box and Lucy to one side.

Kayleigh: It's from Right Ricky.

Lucy: What is?

Kayleigh: The box! Look at the return address.

Lucy: Right Ricky uses a courier service?

Kayleigh: (To Driver) Ricky Davis uses a courier service?

Driver: I work for his dad.

Kayleigh and Lucy: Ah!

Kayleigh: It's addressed to the Head, Miss Collins.

Kayleigh and Lucy look at the box slowly, then drop it like it's hot.

Driver: Can I have a signature please?

Kayleigh: One moment.

Lucy picks up the box gingerly gives it a tentative shake.

Lucy: Ah!

Kayleigh: What?

Lucy: Dunno.

Driver: Come on girls.

Kayleigh: (to Lucy) I'm not signing for it. There's no way I'm signing for a dead gerbil.

Lucy: We don't know it's a dead gerbil. We'll send it back.

Kayleigh: Yeah but what if Right Ricky brings it in to the Head personally. He's hardly gonna check with us first, he'll go in there and see the

Head's secretary and when he's asked why he's brought in a dead rodent it'll all come out it's our fault.

Driver: Girls?

Lucy: We'll sign for it and bin it. We could give it a ceremonial burial or something.

Kayleigh: (Looks around) Where?

Lucy: Over the hedge behind the maths block?

Kayleigh: Okay. No, but it will still be our signature on the form when they look into it.

Driver: Girls!

The girls dither, which inexplicably involves short walks forwards and backwards with the box.

Kayleigh: I've got it.

Kayleigh gets a marker pen from her bag.

Kayleigh: (To Driver) It wasn't actually meant for us. It should be delivered to a Mrs Lavinia Sharp, 14 De Freville Avenue.

Driver: It's not my job.

Kayleigh: Oh come on. It's on your way.

Driver: It's not my job.

Kayleigh: Well we're not signing for it. So unless you get off the premises right now, I'm going to call the police. **(Picks up the phone, and punches buttons)**

Driver: You're kidding me. **(Backs off when she starts speaking)**

Kayleigh: Yes, Hi. This is Kayleigh Black from St Bloos Community College, Milton Road…

Driver: Whatever. **(Looks at address on parcel)**

Exit Driver

Kayleigh: What's that? The time sponsored by Accurist is? **(Looks at watch)** Precisely!

Kayleigh puts phone down.

Lucy: Wow!

Kayleigh: Works every time. Especially on Gran.

The phone rings. Kayleigh picks up.

Kayleigh: Saint Bloos.

Miss Hitchins: Good morning it's Miss Hitchins, can I speak to Brian MacFee?

Kayleigh puts her through.

Mr MacFee (Lucy): MacFee.

Miss Hitchins: Brian it's Rebecca, I have further things to say.

Mr MacFee: (Shouts to unseen boy) Connor watch that javelin boy, you nearly had my eye.

Miss Hitchins: I think that in our five years, we've begun to lose our way.

Mr MacFee: ...and Lewis, take the shot puts out your shirt. **(Mimics holding two shot to his chest)**

Miss Hitchins: (Sl pause) We used to go A La Carte, but now I'm lucky to Go Large.

Mr MacFee: (Ducks) I *did* see you throw that discus Jack, but did you *have* to hit my Vectra?

Miss Hitchins: You used to buy me gifts but now I'm lucky if you share your chips, and do not get me started on our lack of weeks away.

Mr MacFee: We still do things together. I took you off to see Will Young.

Miss Hitchins: He was turning on the Christmas lights, it's not as though he sung!

Mr MacFee: I take you to pop concerts.

Miss Hitchins: Not since Dylan went electric.

Mr MacFee: (Upset) You have no idea what trauma that has caused me down the years. **(SI pause)** But Rebecca I must tell you now, you deserve an explanation, there's a reason for my stinginess, and why we go out less.

Miss Hitchins: Oh!

Mr MacFee: You see I needed to save up, 'cos you deserve a good engagement ring. I was wondering if you'd marry me? Will you honour me with a yes? Ready for the hundred metres? On your marks, get set.

Miss Hitchins: Yes.

At the same time, Mr MacFee sounds a Klaxon that had been behind his back. Miss Hitchins drops her phone.

Kayleigh: I'm starving.

Lucy: Mmm. Do you think we're allowed to eat? **(Gets out a Tupperware box.)**

Kayleigh: What's that then?

Lucy: Bruschetta.

Kayleigh: Brooooshetha. What's wrong with English food?

Lucy: What, like MacDonalds?

Kayleigh: Yeah.

Lucy: (Looks into Kayleigh's carrier bag) So you've got Coke and a Mars Bar. You're not school dinners?

Kayleigh: I used to be free school meals 'til me mum shacked up with Uncle Rob, now we're over the threshold. That and the fact that I'm banned from going within twenty yards of Effin Elsie.

Lucy: Effin Elsie?

Kayleigh: Effin Elsie. She doles out the chips and beans? **(Mimes ladling)** 'Effin Else?'

Lucy stands.

Lucy: I'm just going to get a drink. Do you want anything?

Kayleigh: Na thanks.

Lucy exits. The phone rings. Kayleigh picks it up.

Kayleigh: St Bloos Community College Centre of Excellence. Apart from the Maths department. And English. And Science. And Modern Languages really sucks.

Wendy (Lucy): Hello again, it's Wendy Houghton, Lucy's mother? Can you put me through to Miss Collins please?

Kayleigh: And to what is this appertaining to?

Wendy: It's about Lucy.

Kayleigh: Excellent. **(Finger down on button then up again.) (As Miss Collins)** Miss Collins speaking!

Wendy: Hello again, its Lucy Houghton's mother.

Miss Collins (Kayleigh): Hello again **(Stuck)** Lucy Houghton's mother. Mrs Houghton!

Wendy: Little bit of a panic I'm afraid.

Miss Collins: Uh huh?

Wendy: I've had a phone call just now from Mr Arronson's secretary. He's Lucy's consultant? And he was away for two weeks. When he came back he was furious to discover that his stand-in had overlooked some test results that had come in and were sitting on his desk. Lucy's test results?

Miss Collins: Uh huh? Yeah?

Wendy: So he's now in a blind panic and wants her to come in straight away and they'll wait for a bed to come free and realistically they are going to operate tomorrow, but she'll need to starve herself today for the general anaesthetic?

Miss Collins: Right.

Wendy: So could you possibly get the message to her that she is not to eat for the rest of the day?

Miss Collins: Sure.

Wendy: That's it basically. So I'll keep you informed.

Miss Collins: Yeah. Okay. Er thank you for your call.

Phones down. Lucy wanders back with a bottle of water, a magazine under her arm and bruschetta wedged in her mouth.

Lucy: Alright?

Kayleigh: Yeah.

Kayleigh eyes Lucy warily as she settles with her magazine.

Kayleigh: Er... .

Lucy: Mmmm?

Kayleigh considers her next move.

Kayleigh: Lucy? I'm wondering..

Lucy: What?

Kayleigh: I'm wondering...

Lucy: ...whether I should be stuffing my face with bruschetta when I should be starving myself ready for a general anaesthetic tomorrow? (Pause) That was me on my mobile pretending to be my mum.

Kayleigh: Both times?

Lucy: Uh huh.

Kayleigh: (Shouts) I hate you!

Lucy: (Shouts back gleefully in same tone) We've established that!

Kayleigh: That's outrageous. Of course I didn't believe you for a moment.

Lucy: Of course.

Kayleigh: (Hisses) It's Miss Collins.

Enter the real Miss Collins

Lucy: Yeah right. **(Sees Miss Collins)** It's Miss Collins!

Kayleigh:(Mouths) Ah!

Kayleigh and Lucy: Morning Miss Collins.

Miss Collins: Lucy Houghton and Kayleigh Black. A word.

Miss Collins strolls in front of them. Kayleigh and Lucy sink down.

Miss Collins: I have had an incandescent prospective parent rush in to see me just now, who has been turning my hair grey with tales about how she has been treated today. Someone purporting to be me was rude, unhelpful and I think it is fair to say malicious in the way they treated this member of the community, and she has reported us to the school inspectorate and County Hall. I listened to this poor woman's tale with mounting horror and came to the inescapable conclusion that the perpetrators of the incident were most probably you two girls. What do you have to say for yourselves?

Kayleigh and Lucy: Sorry Miss Collins.

Miss Collins: Impersonating a Headmistress. Sending hate mail to a member of the public.

Kayleigh: It wasn't hate mail; it was a present. Why, did it die or something?

Miss Collins: Be quiet Kayleigh. Now I have more or less managed to calm Mrs Sharp down and I have assured her that you will both be writing letters of apology to her, but the fact remains she has made a formal complaint about us.

Lucy: What's going to happen?

Miss Collins: I shall have to tell them the truth. That two mischievous pupils got up to no good when entrusted with reception. It is hardly a hanging offence. But in the meantime sadly Mrs Sharp has announced that she is no longer interested in sending her daughter to our school. **(Pause)** For which I would like to thank you. **(Winks at them)** It would be very churlish of me not to concede that I do in fact owe you one. Now for heaven's sake try and stay out of trouble for the rest of the term. That means you Kayleigh.

Kayleigh and Lucy: Yes Miss Collins.

Miss Collins almost leaves, Kayleigh sinks with relief.

Lucy: Miss Collins!

Miss Collins: Yes Lucy?

Lucy: When you say you owe us one, do you mean that literally?

Miss Collins: (Laughs) Well...

Lucy: Because there is a favour I would like you to do us. Kayleigh here has applied to RADA and has been down to the auditions. **(Pause)** Did you just smirk?

Kayleigh: (Hisses) Lucy!

Miss Collins: (Grim) Go on.

Lucy: I think she's very talented and I think someone should help her.

Miss Collins: And what did you have in mind Miss Houghton?

Lucy: If for some reason RADA haven't accepted her this time, then perhaps someone could find out why, and what it is they tend to go for. Perhaps someone from the Drama Department could give her some coaching?

Miss Collins: Is this true Kayleigh? You've applied to RADA?

Kayleigh is stony faced and she doesn't make eye contact for an eternity. Miss Collins has had enough and turns to go.

Lucy: Kayleigh!

Kayleigh: (Eventually mumbles) It is what I really want to do.

Miss Collins: (Turns and considers her response) RADA's next auditions are in October, yes?

Kayleigh: How d'you know that?

Miss Collins: I do know my job Miss Black. **(Considers her next move)** Well we could pull you from some of the lessons where you're disruptive, heaven knows everyone will thank me. And I may be able to persuade Miss Dawson from Drama to give you some coaching instead: I think her husband went to RADA. I'm sure between us we will be able to sort something out and give you a fighting chance in October. **(Sarcastic)** Anything else Miss Houghton?

Lucy: No. Thank you Miss Collins.

Miss Collins is smirking as she exits.

PAUSE

Kayleigh: I still hate you.

Lucy: (Surprisingly sad) Yeah well, everyone hates me **(Pause. Then**

surprisingly   cheerful.) Apparently it's
because I have no ass!

**Kayleigh slaps Lucy on her arse with the
magazine.**

Blackout.

About the author:

Paul Vincent is the author of several novels including, 'The Textbook Man' and 'Free', and the non fiction title '50 Things You Can Do Today To Beat Depression.'

Printed in the United Kingdom
by Lightning Source UK Ltd.
107925UKS00001B/512

9 781846 850318